You've Got What It Takes!

You've Got What It Takes!

Sondra's Tips for Making Your Dreams Come True

Sondra Clark

with some help from Silvana Clark

Fleming H. Revell
A Division of Baker Book House Co
Grand Rapids, Michigan 49516

Published by Fleming H. Revell
a division of Baker Book House Company
P.O. Box 6287, Grand Rapids, MI 49516-6287

Printed in the United States of America

Library of Congress Cataloging-in-Publication Data

Clark, Sondra.
    You've got what it takes! : Sondra's tips for making your dreams come true / Sondra Clark with Silvana Clark.
       p.   cm.
    Summary: Twelve-year-old Sondra, whose first book was published when she was in third grade and who is "spokeschild" for Childcare International, shares tips on how to set goals, take responsible risks, and achieve success.
    ISBN 0–8007–5836–6 (pbk.)
    1. Success—Juvenile literature. [1. Success. 2. Goal (Psychology).
3. Children's writings.] I. Clark, Silvana. II. Title.
BJ1611.2 .C49 2002
158.1—dc21   2002004087

Sondra gives a portion of the proceeds from this book to Childcare International, www.childcare-intl.org

For current information about all releases from Baker Book House, visit our web site:
http://www.bakerbooks.com

Thank you Jerry Chambers, for your part in getting Chevy to donate a truck for us so we can travel around the United States for a year promoting Childcare International. Because of your help, children in developing countries will get sponsors and be able to go to school and live better lives.

Thanks, Dad, for being a wonderful father. You inspire me with your great ideas and positive attitude. You are always there to help me make my dreams come true. Thanks, also, for building me a life-size horse in my room when my dream was to own a horse! I love you!

Contents

Introduction

Sondra's Story

Do you remember the first time you tried to stand on your head? If you are like me, your legs flopped back and forth and you quickly fell over. Some of you kept trying and trying until finally you could get your feet in the air and keep them there for a few seconds. Standing on your head was possible—if you gave it plenty of effort. As kids, we sometimes like things to come easily to us. Wouldn't it be great if we could all instantly learn our addition and subtraction facts? Just think how fun it would be to pick up a clarinet for the first time and instantly be able to play in the school marching band.

Anything is possible if you work hard at it. For example, let's pretend you are a Girl Scout and want to sell the most Girl Scout cookies in your area. You might have this conversation with your dad:

9

You: "Dad! Dad! Guess what!"

Dad: "You sound excited. What's up?"

You: "I've decided to work really hard to sell lots and lots of Girl Scout cookies."

Dad: "Seems like a great idea."

You: "Yes, I'm going to be the top cookie seller. That's what I'm going to do!"

What would happen if you went and watched TV after that conversation? Would it be possible for you to sell cookies if you never even walked through the neighborhood to sell cookies? No, you would need to make a plan to reach your goal. It might look something like this:

1. Find out what last year's record was for selling cookies.
2. Find out the exact days of the sale.
3. Make a list of possible places where you could sell cookies and people you could sell them to.
4. Have an adult give you suggestions.
5. Write a "contract" with yourself about how many cookies you'll sell every day.
6. Make sure to let your troop leader know your plans so she can order extra cookies for you.
7. Start selling!

Now let's pretend you want to be a professional soccer player. That's certainly possible, but what do you think you would have to do before you could become famous as a super soccer player? Even if playing soccer is not your goal, try this simple exercise: Make a list of five things you might need to do to become a professional soccer star.

Five things I would need to do starting right now if I wanted to become a famous soccer player:

1.

2.

3.

4.

5.

Now write down a goal of your own. It may be as simple as learning a new song on the piano or as challenging as becoming an astronaut.

My goal is: _____

_____

Take a few minutes to list what you need to do to reach your very own specific goal. Don't worry about the order—just list some steps.

Things I need to do starting right now if I want to reach my goal:

1.

2.

3.

4.

5.

You can see how simply having a few steps to take will help you reach your goal. Naturally it also means you have to give some extra effort.

I'd like to share about something I did that took a lot of work. My mom has written several books. One day when I was eight years old, I asked her, "Mom, can I write a book?" She said, "Sure, but you have to write about something you know about." As a kid, I didn't know too much about brain surgery or mechanical engineering. Since I did craft projects all the time, I decided to write a book about crafts. My mom thought that was a good idea. I made a project and then dictated the steps to my mother. She wrote them down and read back my directions. Then I made the project over again, following the instructions exactly to make sure they were clear. Sometimes I'd have to change the steps or describe the process another way.

I started this project at the beginning of winter break when I was in third grade. I set a goal of writing four pages a day during my twelve days of vacation. At the end of the break, how many pages were done? (I hope you said forty-eight!) I set a goal of writing two pages a day during the rest of January. That meant the book was written in about six weeks. I called the book *Craft Fun with Sondra,* and it describes more than fifty-five arts and crafts projects. Sure, there were times when I didn't want to work on it, but I knew that getting the book published was possible only if I gave my best effort. My mom helped me find a literary agent, and she sold it to a publisher. I became an author!

Since the book came out, I've had all sorts of exciting experiences. Some of the money I've made goes to Bethany Services, a national Christian adoption agency, to help kids get adopted. I also get to fly around the United States and be on TV shows. I must admit it's fun when I get picked up at the airport in a limousine! But then I come home and still have to do homework and chores.

After I saw that it was possible to write one book, I wrote another book when I was nine called *Wearable Art with Sondra.* I wrote it more or less the same way as *Craft Fun with Sondra.* That meant I made a lot of craft projects! I'm really excited about this book, because a portion of the proceeds goes to Childcare International, a relief organization that offers people in the United States an opportunity to sponsor a child in Africa, India, or Haiti for thirty dollars a month.

Childcare International asked me to be a "spokeschild," and I spent my last Christmas vacation in Africa filming a documentary for them. While I was in Kenya and Uganda, I visited schools that had no water or electricity. We took along all sorts of craft supplies to give the kids I met. At one school, about fifty kids sat at benches while my parents and I passed out paper and new markers so they could draw pictures. They all understood English, so I was surprised when they just quizzically stared at us. I said, "Go ahead, color a picture." They still looked at the markers and me. Finally, my mom and I understood. They had never seen markers and didn't know how to take the caps off to color. They also had never seen glue or scissors before. It was amazing to me that kids my age lived with so few "things." There were no toys, no extra clothes, and certainly no television. I had planned to bring my sponsored child a new backpack. I'm glad I didn't, because she had nothing to put in it! I brought her markers, colored papers, paints, and new clothes instead. You can see more about Childcare International on their web site, www.childcare-intl.org

What is exciting about setting goals to achieve your dream is that you never know what will happen. Maybe your dream is to design computer programs. Who knows, Bill Gates might even call you up and ask for advice! What's your dream? Hopefully this book will help you find your dream—or *dreams*—and then give you the steps to see those dreams come true.

I'm sure all of you have ideas about things you want to do or be. Ask your parents to tell you about Henry David Thoreau. He came up with many profound thoughts, including this one:

"It's all right to build your castles in the air. Now put foundations under them."

That means it's wonderful to want to be a ballet dancer, write your own book, start a pet-walking business, or become president. But those ideas need "foundations" like goals and effort to become real. For example, after setting the foundation for becoming a ballet dancer by taking dance lessons, you might find yourself teaching ballet to preschoolers or designing ballet costumes.

Once you set the foundation, anything can happen. Get ready for a fun time as you read this book and start building some foundations!

The Olympic Torch

The crowd is cheering! They're calling my name! I feel as if I just won an Olympic gold medal! Except I'm not an Olympic athlete. I did get to take part in a 2002 Olympic activity. Because of my work with Childcare International, I was selected to be an Olympic torchbearer. You might have watched the torchbearers on TV. They carried the Olympic flame through forty-six different states. Out of 11,000 runners, I was the youngest. In order to be selected, you had to have done something inspirational. The Olympic committee received 210,000 applications. Evidently they felt my work in helping AIDs orphans in Africa was inspirational enough to get selected as a torchbearer.

While getting ready to carry the torch in Seattle, I rode in a van with Megan Quann. At 16, she competed in swimming at the 2000 Olympics. She knows what it means to work hard to reach a goal. Megan gets up at 4:30 every morning so she can swim for a few hours before school. Then after school she does weight training and conditioning. Her work paid off, because she earned two gold medals.

Getting out of the Olympic van, I felt incredibly nervous. The group leader said, "Sondra, just remember. Right now, you are the only person in the world that is carrying the Olympic torch." Yikes! Because I was the youngest torchbearer, there were extra camera crews and photographers following me. There were also four policemen on motorcycles, a helicopter flying overhead, a security truck behind me, and a film crew in a truck in front of me. Oh, yes. I also had my grandmother racing alongside, trying to take pictures. She even bumped into a cameraman since he couldn't run as fast as she did!

It felt amazing to be representing America as well as the Olympic spirit. The side of the torch says, "Light the Fire Within." I think that means that each one of us can light our own personal flame inside and make our dreams come true. Now I go around to schools and other community groups, displaying my torch and getting people excited about how they can "Light the Fire Within" in their own lives.

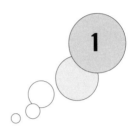

What's Your Dream?

Dream

Dream up your fantasy
Think about your future,
Wish upon a falling star,
Daydream to your destiny.
—Sondra

What do you want to do with your life? That may seem like a silly question, since you're probably busy thinking about your math test and the sleepover coming up this weekend. This isn't the time to decide what college to attend or to pick a career, but you can learn some skills about how to be successful as a preteen girl. You can set goals and make plans for things that are important to you right now.

See the list on page 18. Are there things you like to do?

Things I Like to Do

☆ I like listening to music.

☆ I like building things.

☆ I like being outdoors.

☆ I like playing a musical instrument.

☆ I like playing sports.

☆ I like painting and drawing.

☆ I like doing volunteer work.

☆ I like doing science experiments.

☆ I like designing clothes.

☆ I like being with my family.

☆ I like hearing about what missionaries do.

☆ I like working with young children.

☆ I like being around animals.

☆ I like having new experiences.

☆ I like being alone sometimes.

☆ I like being the center of attention.

☆ I like having the same routine every day.

☆ I like doing arts and crafts projects.

You probably checked many of those categories. Great! Most kids have a lot of different interests, and sometimes those interests change from week to week. Remember when you were four years old and wanted to be a ballerina when you grew up? Your mother probably enrolled you in a dance class, and soon you were prancing around the dance studio. The next week you decided you wanted to be a horseback rider. You soon pranced around the house on your stick horse. Your parents knew it was important to "explore" different roles. Now that you're older, it's still important to explore different possibilities. You obviously need to be more selective, however, because you can't sign up for drama, drop it, take up skiing, drop that, and then take up rock climbing—all in one month. You can find out about the "big world out there" in easier ways.

Are you interested in scuba diving? Call your local YMCA or scuba store and ask if they have a one-time scuba lesson. Then you can see if you like being underwater without making a major commitment. Read books on different topics. Maybe you want to start raising butterflies. The Internet has many sites that give information about how to attract butterflies to your backyard. The point is, God has given us a wonderful world to explore. Until we're old enough to actually take off and explore foreign countries, we can use resources around us. Don't be afraid to talk to your science teacher about what it takes to teach science. If you enjoy doing crafts, check with artists about how they make a living as a professional crafter.

Would you like to eat the same meal three times a day every day for a week? Probably not. You've heard the saying, "Variety is the spice of life." Try to add some variety to your life by being open to new possibilities. Our family goes on "educational experiences." These are "mystery trips" where someone finds a totally new (and inexpensive) activity or event for us to enjoy. It works like this: Someone in the family says, "We're going on an educational experience tomorrow at 7:00 P.M." The other family members know they have to be ready to go to an unknown location for a new experience. Since the event is something we've never done before, no one can complain. The point is to experience something that we normally wouldn't do.

My parents have taken me on some unusual educational experiences. We've visited gas refineries and joined seniors in playing bingo. One night my mom had us take flashlights and walk through the dark woods at night to see an evening craft bazaar. Another time my parents told me we were going on a "hot" educational experience. It was hot and crazy! We drove to Western Washington University, our local college. There we saw a group perform stunts with fire. They threw fiery torches, swallowed flaming swords, and jumped over flaming ropes. At the end "Flame Boy" wore a special suit, doused himself with gasoline, and was set on fire. His whole body was on fire! Another less exciting educational experience was when a hardware store had "Ladies Night" before Christmas. My mom and I had a great time browsing the tool aisle while eating fudge and sipping cider with dozens of other women.

Step into Action ------------------------→

Talk to your family about educational experiences. Would they be open to trying a few? Finding inexpensive events to attend is fun. Just listen to the radio or look in the paper for activities, such as a model railroad demonstration or a new art gallery opening. Perhaps you could have one educational experience a month for the next three months. It's a good way for the whole family to expand their horizons.

Sometimes going on educational experiences feels funny, because we are "out of our comfort zone." We usually don't know the people involved, and we're unsure of what is going to happen. Yet as we look back on all the unique things we've done, our family is glad we took risks and went on educational experiences.

★**Real Life Example from Sondra**★

Every once in a while I've thought about being a veterinarian. Last month I asked a local veterinarian if I could watch her perform an operation. She agreed, and I arrived on time to watch her perform surgery on a cat. It was fascinating to see her anesthetize the cat. She actually had rock and roll music blaring over the radio as she operated. She said the operation would take ten minutes. After nine and a half minutes, I started to feel hot and dizzy. Suddenly I fainted! I guess I'm not cut out to be a veterinarian!

Be creative in following your dream. If you think you want to be a kindergarten teacher, ask if you can help teach a kindergarten Sunday school class. You may find out you have a talent for working with young children. (Or you may find out you don't like being around little kids!)

"Silly Quiz"

You want to be a dancer on Broadway. Check all the things that might be logical to do.

○ Pack up your suitcase and take a bus to New York.
○ Nail boards on your bedroom floor so you can practice tap dancing.

21

○ When your math teacher gets boring, jump out of your seat and start doing dance moves around the room. (You have to practice somewhere.)

○ Always wear a tutu, even if you go to the mall. You never know when a Broadway director will see you.

○ Take a few dance classes at the local YWCA or recreation department.

○ Audition for parts in the *Nutcracker* or other local dance productions.

Hopefully you won't pack your bags and head to New York until you get older. For now, concentrate on the at-home, practical things you can do to find out more about your interests.

Step into Action ─ ─ ─ ─ ─ ─ ─ ─ ─ ─ ─ ─ ─ ─ →

Have you thought about being a fashion designer or computer programmer? Ask an adult to help you find someone who has a job you are interested in. Call them up and ask if you can "job shadow" them. That means you will follow them around for a day (or a few hours) and see what they do. You may find out the job isn't as glamorous as you thought. (You may even find yourself fainting!)

Many kids have far-fetched ideas about what they want to do or be. Of course, it's important to dream, but you also need to be realistic. If you live in the middle of the desert in Arizona, it might be hard to become an expert downhill skier. But nothing can stop you from reading about skiing or watching skiers on television. You could even become pen pals with someone who lives in Colorado and skis all the time. The main thing is to explore different possibilities about what you enjoy doing.

Sometimes our plans are limited by age restrictions. For example, no matter how much you want to get your driver's license, you won't be able to reach your goal until you are the legal driving age for your state. But in the meantime you can learn about road signs, speed limits, and safety rules. Just don't take your mom or dad's car out for a spin when you are underage!

As you explore different possibilities in your life, you can learn how to make some dreams come true by setting short-term goals. You can learn how to do that in the next chapter.

★Real Life Example from Sondra★

When we got back from Africa, my parents and I started dreaming about how we could help the children we met in Africa. Our dream focused on traveling around the United States in an RV, to places where I could speak at different churches and raise money for Childcare International. We dreamed, we prayed, and we contacted Jerry Chambers at Chambers Chevrolet in Bellingham, where we live. On my birthday Mr. Chambers called up and said, "Happy Birthday, Sondra! Chevrolet would like to give you a new truck to use for a year as you travel around the country." Now that's a dream come true!

23

Reach Your Goals One Step at a Time

Have you heard adults tell you, "Work hard to achieve your goal"? Sure you know about making a goal in football, but just exactly what is a goal? Let's get technical. The *Encarta College Dictionary* says a goal is "something that somebody wants to achieve." That means your goal could be as complicated as discovering a cure for AIDS or simply wanting to turn your book report in on time.

Most of us think about what we want to do but don't take action. Can you imagine someone wanting to be an Olympic figure skater but never even trying to ice skate? To better understand goals, let's start with short-term goals, plans you have that take less time than long-term goals. That's why they're called "short term!" And they are usually easier to accomplish. A long-term goal might be to become a marine biologist after you graduate from college in ten years. This means you need to take science classes, do an internship at Sea World, and meet other marine biologists. Short-term goals most often happen in a few weeks or less.

Examples of Short-term Goals

✮ You want to get an A on next week's math test.

✮ You decide to learn to play a new song on the piano.

✮ You plan to finish reading the four Gospels in the Bible.

✮ You try to earn money to buy a new CD.

✮ You plan a friend's surprise birthday party.

Mia Hamm had this to say about goal setting: "I've worked too hard and too long to let anything stand in the way of my goals. I will not let my teammates down or let myself down."

One of the best ways to be successful at reaching long-term goals is to practice with easier goals. Short-term goals are "stepping stones" to long-term goals. After all, if you set a goal to attend a one-day soccer camp, you may be on your way to becoming the next Mia Hamm!

Why not practice reaching a short-term goal this week? Think of something you'd like to accomplish within seven to ten days. It doesn't have to be spectacular. The idea is to understand what you need to do to reach your goal and then *take action!*

Some Short-term Goals

✮ Being consistent about cleaning your hamster cage

☆ Participating more in math class, even though you feel math is not your strongest subject
☆ Using your alarm clock so you're not late for school
☆ Having daily devotions consistently
☆ Practicing the piano at least ten minutes a day
☆ Making a new friend
☆ Designing a new craft project

Try some of these steps to set a short-term goal:

1. *Be specific about your goal.* It's easy to say, "I want to be a better basketball player by the time practice starts next month." But what does that mean? Do you want to be better than your five-year-old sister or better than Michael Jordan? You should be specific by saying, "I want to make at least five baskets out of every ten free throws I shoot." You can make a chart that shows exactly how many free throws you did make. Instead of saying, "My short-term goal is to be 'nice' to the new girl at school," be specific. What does "nice" mean? Will you eat lunch with her? Will you invite her to your church youth group? Figure out exactly what you will do to be nice to her.

Here's one short-term goal I have:

Great! You have a short-term goal. Now go on to step 2.

2. *Set a date to reach your goal.* Again, just saying, "I'm going to be nice to the new girl" doesn't give you the guidelines you need. Figure out a reasonable amount of time to reach your goal.

It could be something like this: "I'm going to eat lunch with Trina every day next week. Then next weekend I'll ask her to come to Middle School Madness at church with me. That way she'll get to meet a lot of kids and feel comfortable."

Another way to look at a date is to say, "Two weeks from today I plan to have earned twelve dollars for the earrings I want to buy at Jane's Jewelry Shop."

How long will it take to reach your short-term goal? Write the dates below.

I plan to start working on my goal on: _____

I will reach my goal on: _____

3. *Write down your daily steps.* Get a blank calendar or a piece of paper. Mark out the days available to reach your short-term goal. Write down what you'll do on a daily basis. Let's go back to the free-throw example. Pretend your goal is to make five baskets from the free-throw line for every ten tries. It's easy to come up with excuses why you can't work on reaching your goals.

Some Excuses NOT to Use

★ I can't practice basketball today because the sun is too bright.

☆ I can't practice basketball today because there isn't enough sun.

☆ My ball is too round.

☆ I have to read the entire Bible tonight.

☆ I might get too much exercise.

☆ My dog is sleeping in the driveway, and I might trip over him if I practice.

☆ I can't practice; my favorite television show is on.

☆ I can't practice; I'm depressed because my favorite television show isn't on!

Naturally you wouldn't reach your short-term goal using those flimsy excuses. Try writing ideas like this for each day:

Daily Schedule to Reach Short-term Goal

Monday:	Practice free throws for fifteen minutes. Record how many baskets I make.
Tuesday:	Stay after school and ask Coach Edwards to help me.
Wednesday:	Challenge my dad to a free-throw contest, which will motivate me to practice.
Thursday:	Practice twenty-five minutes in school gym . . . and so on.

4. *Take action!* See? You've just come up with a specific goal and set a completion date. Now comes the hard part. You actually have to do something to reach your goal. Yup! You have to work! Sometimes we get so excited about

29

⭐**Real Life Example from Sondra**⭐

I used to race around the house in the morning looking for my books, backpack, and lunch. My mom wasn't much help. All she said was, "Maybe you should get your things together the night before." I made a short-term goal to get more organized for mornings. Every night before bed I'd put all my things in my backpack (except my lunch) and set it by the front door. If I had orchestra, I'd set out my violin too. Now in the mornings I just pick up my things and walk out to catch the bus. That goal made my mornings less chaotic.

writing our goals that we forget it takes action to fulfill those goals.

After you've written a daily schedule, get busy! Make a point of taking time to do what you said you would. It might mean less TV or less telephone time.

Having a daily schedule will keep you focused. You can cross out each day's plan after you're done. I like using a felt-tip marker and writing, "DONE!" after I'm finished with each task. Then when I have the calendar filled with black writing, I know I've done what I could do to reach my goal.

Review Time

The steps to reaching a short-term goal are easy:

1. Be specific about what you want to do.
2. Set dates to begin and reach your goal.
3. Write down daily steps to reach the goal.
4. Take action! Work on reaching your goal.

Now that you are a "champion short-term goal setter," you're ready to move on to long-term goals, goals that involve more time and effort. Since long-term goals take longer to reach, we'd better get started!

Big Dreams Take Big Plans

3

Does it seem like years until your next birthday? Adults always say time passes quickly, but kids often feel that time drags on and on. When you're only twelve or thirteen, going to college seems like an eternity away. Most of the time you'll be planning short-term goals, like auditioning for the school play or earning spending money for camp. If you are truly ambitious and want to plan for the future, here are some tips.

Since you already know how to set short-term goals, you are well on your way to planning for long-term goals and dreams.

Some Long-term Goals

- ✯ Going to college
- ✯ Learning to pilot a plane
- ✯ Becoming a missionary in Africa
- ✯ Becoming an paleontologist and looking for dinosaur bones
- ✯ Training a dog for television commercials (That's what my mom did!)
- ✯ Writing songs and putting out a CD
- ✯ Buying your parents a new house (They'll like that goal!)
- ✯ Becoming a professional scuba diver
- ✯ Writing a book

As you can see, long-term goals take more time and effort than short-term goals. In fact, they usually require several years of preparation and work. But first you need to know what it is you want to accomplish. That's a lesson Alice learned in *Alice in Wonderland.*

One day Alice came to a fork in the road and saw a Cheshire cat sitting in a tree. Alice asked, "Which road do I take?"

"Where do you want to go?" asked the cat.

"I don't know," Alice replied.

"Then it doesn't matter which road you take," said the cat.

The point is, you'll waste a lot of time and get nowhere unless you have a plan. A plan will help you decide what you need to do, whether you need money to meet your goal, and how long it will take to accomplish your goal. So get a plan and get into action! You probably watched sixteen-year-old Sarah Hughes win a gold medal in figure skating at the

2002 Olympics. The TV stations often ran a home movie of her as a young skater. She's standing on the ice as an adorable seven-year-old and says, "When I grow up, my dream is to win the gold medal in the Olympics in figure skating." She knew exactly what she wanted to do. After years of hard work, her dream came true.

At first you may have larger-than-life plans for meeting your long-term goal. Then reality sets in. Who will drive you to classes? Who will pay for instructors or equipment? Do you have the time to practice? Here are some ways to successfully reach your long-term goal.

Five Ways to Reach a Goal

Have you studied the five Ws of effective writing? Your teacher has probably told you that you need to answer five questions when writing a report: Who? What? Why? When? and How? (Okay, these aren't five Ws, but it's easier than saying "the four Ws and one H.")

You can use those same guidelines when setting goals. As you consider what you want to do, fill in the blanks.

Who:_____
  Usually this means yourself, with occasional help
  from a friend or an adult.

What: _____
  What do you want to do? Be specific.

Why: _____
  Why do you want to do this? To impress your

friends? To help other people? If you really want to do this, you'll work harder.

When: _____

By what date do you want to finish your goal? Having a completion date gives you focus. It also stops you from saying, "I'll work on this tomorrow . . . or the next day . . . or the next day." Be realistic though. If you want to run a marathon but get tired running around the block, you won't want to sign up for next week's marathon.

How: _____

This is the most important. How will you reach your goal? How will you find money? Time? Supplies and equipment? Adult help? Transportation?

After you figure out the who, what, why, when, and how, you'll have a better idea of how to actually reach your goal.

When considering the "when" in reaching your goal, set up a series of small goals leading to your long-term goal. For example, say it's nearly February and your long-term goal is to run a twenty-six-mile marathon with your dad in September. You could list the dates like this:

Feb 5:   Read a book on how to train for a marathon.

Feb 25:   Start jogging daily for at least one mile.

March: Enter a 5K road run put on by the Parks and Recreation Department.

April: Take a class in long-distance running techniques.

Set a short-term goal each month to prepare yourself for reaching your long-term goal of running the marathon in September.

Don't forget to set up little rewards for yourself as you go along. Reaching a goal is hard work, but it shouldn't be drudgery. Celebrate when you are halfway to your goal. Ask your parents if they'll throw you an ice cream party if you reach your long-term goal on the designated day.

Step into Action ------------------→

Ask a parent, teacher, or older brother or sister if they've ever had a long-term goal. Ask them if they achieved their goal. What would they have done differently? What did they learn from the process of trying to reach a goal? You'll discover that different people go about achieving their goals in different ways. And maybe you'll find some helpful ways to meet your own goals.

Bridges to Success

Think about a bridge. Bridges are used to help you get from one side of a canyon, river, or street to the other side. You take "steps" to cross the bridge. In the same way, consider the steps you want to take to reach your goal.

Let's say you want to convince your parents to let you get a dog. You'd love a cute, furry puppy, but you know that it means a commitment of caring for the dog for maybe as long as twelve to fifteen years. Your "Bridge of Goals" might look like this:

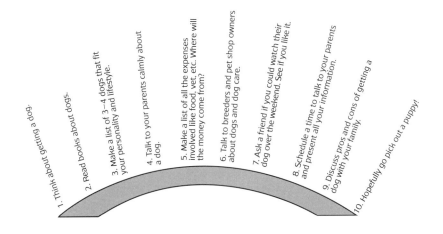

1. Think about getting a dog.
2. Read books about dogs.
3. Make a list of 3–4 dogs that fit your personality and lifestyle.
4. Talk to your parents calmly about a dog.
5. Make a list of all the expenses involved like food, vet, etc. Where will the money come from?
6. Talk to breeders and pet shop owners about dogs and dog care.
7. Ask a friend if you could watch their dog over the weekend. See if you like it.
8. Schedule a time to talk to your parents and present all your information.
9. Discuss pros and cons of getting a dog with your family.
10. Hopefully go pick out a puppy!

Take into consideration that your parents may have logical reasons for not allowing you to get a dog. Does your dad have horrible allergies when he's close to a dog? Would a Great Dane fit into your apartment? Would the dog be home alone all day? All these factors go into making a decision. If you take the time to show your parents how you've thought through the five Ws and made a bridge of goals, they'll most likely seriously consider your request.

Six Ways to "See" Your Goal Come True

★ 1. Write down on a piece of paper what you want to do. Put it by the mirror so you can see it when you brush your hair.

★ 2. Cut pictures out of magazines and make a collage of your goal.

★ 3. Use the computer to make a sign that says something to encourage you in reaching your goal, such as "Future Marine Biologist!" or "Finish Reading *Gone with the Wind* by December 1st!"

☆ 4. Write your goal on four or five Post-it notes and stick them throughout the house where you'll see them.

☆ 5. Incorporate your goal into a screensaver. (Check with others if you share a computer.)

★Real Life Example from Sondra★

Writing a book is certainly a long-term goal. To help me reach my goal when writing my first book, I made up an official-looking contract on the computer. I left space so my parents and I could sign it. It looked like this:

I, Sondra Clark, plan to write a craft book with 50 projects. I will do one page a day, beginning on July 1, 2000, and finish on August 20.

Sondra _____

Allan _____

Silvana _____

Then I posted the contract where I could see it. When I didn't feel like working on the book, I looked at the contract, and it motivated me to write that one page.

✫ 6. Draw or paint a picture showing you achieving your goal.

Congratulations! Now you know how to set short- and long-term goals. Let's look at some other practical ways to help you become a successful person so you can make your dreams come true.

The Power of Being Positive

D o you ever wonder why some kids get As on tests without ever really trying while you struggle to get a B? Do you ever wish you had more friends? Do you want to be selected for school leadership positions? Would you like to be an officer in your church youth group?

As you think about these questions, it's reassuring to know that other girls are thinking the same kinds of things. They may wonder why you are so good at basketball or singing in the church choir. While some people just naturally have more talent in one area than others, a large part of success is having a positive attitude.

You've probably heard people talk about the "glass half full" theory. This uncomplicated theory really makes sense. Go into the kitchen and fill a glass halfway with water. Look at the glass. Is the glass half full or half empty? Ask other family members what they think. Most people with positive attitudes see the glass as half *full* of water. If you're thirsty, you'll at least have something to drink. A negative person, however, might say, "That glass doesn't have much water. It's almost empty."

Recently our pastor told a story about two young brothers. One was always happy and positive; the other complained about everything. On Christmas morning the negative boy ripped open his presents and said things like, "I don't like the color of that car" and "I wanted a bigger bike." The boy with a positive attitude was told to go to the garage for his present. He ran to the garage and found it full of manure—stinky, gross manure! A few minutes later his dad went out to the garage and found the boy shoveling the manure. "Dad!" he shouted, "with all this manure, I'm sure there's a pony in here somewhere!" That is a silly story, but it does show us that you can look for the good in any situation.

Olympic gymnast Mary Lou Retton said this about being a positive person: "I never pictured myself crashing or falling off the beam. I always pictured myself doing my routine perfectly."

First Thessalonians 5:18 says, "In everything give thanks" (NKJV). When I was nine, I had to go to a specialist because of some weird stomach problems I was having. In order for the tests to work, I couldn't eat for twenty-four hours beforehand. In fact, my dad took my mouth-watering sandwich out of my hands and said, "Sorry, we just made a doctor's appointment. No food for twenty-four hours." He plopped down two sports drinks and told me they were lunch, dinner, and breakfast combined. At first it wasn't too bad, but after a few hours, I got hungry! My parents helped by skipping dinner so I wouldn't have to see them eat. (I think my dad snuck popcorn after I went to bed.)

Twenty-four hours later I was famished! I walked by the hospital cafeteria and saw pasta, pizza, and pie. I could only look and smell. My mom got me some lunch—a cup of thin chicken broth. No noodles, no vegetables, no chicken. Just plain watery broth. I could have looked at the broth and said, "This isn't lunch. I need a double cheeseburger!" Or I could have used the glass half full theory and said, "It's not much, but it smells good and has some flavor."

Now, three years later, when I think of that cup of broth, it seems like the best meal I ever had. The flavor was intense, and the warm liquid felt good going down my throat. I learned that it's better to look for the positive side of each situation.

Here are three ways to develop a positive attitude:

1. *Think positive thoughts.* It's easy to say, "I can't ever learn to skateboard. I'm too clumsy." Instead, tell yourself, "Skateboarding is fun. I'll keep trying, and soon I'll be able to keep my balance." The Bible tells us in Philippians 4:8, "Fix your thoughts on what is true and good and right. . . . Think about all you can praise God for and be glad about" (TLB). Lisa Taylor Parsi performs with Circus Smirkus, a traveling circus made up of students. She enjoys performing on the high wire. Lisa says, "You can accomplish any goal as long as you have a positive attitude." She has to stay positive as she hops, dances, and turns on a thin wire up in the air.

2. *Make a decision to be a positive person.* We have already learned about the glass half full theory; now let's learn

about the self-fulfilling prophecy theory. It goes along with the phrase, "If you believe it, you can achieve it." That means that if you believe in something strongly enough, you can reach success. You probably won't win your campaign for student council representative if you say, "No one will vote for me. Why should I put up campaign signs? I won't even practice my speech, because no one will vote for me anyway." With that negative attitude, it would be difficult to get people excited about voting for you. On the other hand, you could decide to be positive. You could

* Put up posters decorated with bright colors.
* Make campaign buttons using colorful paper or even pieces of candy.
* Work on writing a speech that gets everyone's attention. (See chapter 10 in this book for great ideas on speech writing.)
* Ask friends to help you.
* Keep a positive, upbeat attitude throughout the campaign.
* Come up with a catchy slogan, such as, "There's no match for Mandy Hatch." "When Leslie's the one, consider it done." I saw a great campaign slogan by a boy named Logan. He wrote, "Vote for Logan . . . he needs no slogan."

3. *Surround yourself with positive people.* Ever notice how you feel good when you are around people who are happy and positive? They lift you up and help you see the good in life. In the same way, if you are around people who complain

★Real Life Example from Sondra★

Because we had moved, I started middle school at a school where I knew only four or five people. It was scary going to a new school and not having my usual group of friends to hang out with. I decided to keep a positive attitude and try to meet new people. I ran for sixth-grade president because people would then at least know who I was from my speech. I didn't win the election, but I did get to know a lot of people because of my campaign. By the way, my slogan was "Make your mark . . . next to Clark."

and cut other people down, you'll soon find yourself becoming negative too.

Make an effort to be positive. Your self-fulfilling prophecy will help you to look for the good in other people and in your life. It sure beats sitting around moping and singing that favorite camp song:

Nobody likes me, everybody hates me,
I'm gonna eat some worms.
Long, slim, slimy ones,
Short, fat, juicy ones,
Itsy bitsy, fuzzy-wuzzy worms!

45

Step into Action - - - - - - - - - - - - - - →

Try this activity to help you remember the importance of having a positive attitude. Write down the number in the alphabet that each letter represents. (A=1, B=2, C=3)

A_____

T_____

T_____

I_____

T_____

U_____

D_____

E_____

_____ Add the numbers. What do you get?

"One hundred percent of your success is determined by your attitude."

Keep up that positive attitude, and soon you'll be on your way to reaching your dreams.

How to Be a Smile Maker

As kids, we often don't realize how hard adults work to make our lives better. They teach us, buy us things, and cheer us up when we're sad. Now it's our turn to start thinking about how we can make other people's lives brighter.

Bringing cheer can be as simple as playing a game with your younger brother to help him forget the pain after he skins his knee. You could even decorate his Band-Aid.

Do you pay attention to how your parents are feeling at the end of the day? They probably ask how your day went. But do you show an interest in the events of their day? Perhaps your mom's computer crashed and destroyed all her files. She may need your understanding. Take the time to show an interest in other people. This might come as a shock, but the world doesn't revolve around you! Try being a person other people want to be with.

Which one of these people would you like to be around?
Someone who

always talks about herself

is always bragging

complains about everything

cuts down other people

is sarcastic

is rude to adults

doesn't contribute positive ideas

Or someone who

is polite

tries to include other people

makes jokes

is positive

contributes ideas

listens to other people's ideas

tells what she's done without cutting other people down

Obviously it's more fun to be around the second person.
Kids have an obligation not to always "take" in a relationship. Babies don't know any better. They demand attention,
food, or a toy *right now!* They don't think about other people and their needs. But we're not babies.

Think about your parents and other adults in your life.
They all make an effort to see that you have what you need.
My dad's favorite fifth grade teacher made an effort to teach

★Real Life Example from Sondra★

I've played soccer since I was five years old. My dad was my coach for four years. In Washington, soccer season is usually windy, rainy, and cold! My dad would bring a small tent to the games. He had sleeping bags and a thermos of hot chocolate inside. When our team wasn't playing, we could go inside the tent to get warm. We all appreciated his extra effort.

in an interesting way. One day the teacher stood on his head and ate a banana to make a point. My dad can't remember what the point was, but he sure was impressed that his teacher made the effort to stand on his head!

Were you sad recently? Did your parents comfort you and go out of their way to make you feel better? Maybe you lost an important soccer game and felt bad. Your parents probably said encouraging things to you. Maybe they even took you out for ice cream. They thought about you, not about the fact that they had been standing in the wind and rain on the sidelines watching you play. We need to return respect by giving back to other people.

You can give back to others in many ways:

★ 1. When your mom comes home from a business trip, have the house clean for her.

★ 2. Let your parents have some time together before barging in and asking for a ride to the mall.

★ 3. Celebrate National Appreciate Your Teacher Week in November by doing nice things for your teacher.

★ 4. Give your parents "I Love You" coupons. Make up coupons for vacuuming the car or sweeping the garage.

★ 5. Look at and listen to your parents when they tell you about "the good old days."

Your New Job

As you get older, you'll fill out applications asking your name, address, and occupation. Occupation? You might not think you have an occupation, but how very wrong you are. Your occupation could include student, daughter, soccer player, pianist, actor, mathematician, friend, or something else.

Why not come up with a new occupation of "smile maker"? No, you don't have to be the class clown or act goofy all the time. Just look for ways to add some fun and laughter to the people around you. Annette Goodheart lists some benefits of laughing in her book *Laughter Therapy.* Laughing

★ helps you reduce stress
★ puts problems in perspective
★ exercises your cardiovascular system
★ makes other people feel good

★Real Life Example from Sondra★

My dad was going commercial fishing in Alaska for four weeks. Before he left, I wanted to make him something special to wear when he got cold and wet catching salmon. He always wears hooded sweatshirts on the boat, so I made him a "Daddy Deerest" shirt. I used fabric paint and my footprint for the head of the deer and my hands for the antlers. Every time he wore the shirt, he was reminded that I love him. I knew the shirt would make him smile.

Making a "Deer Dad" or "Deer Mom" Shirt

Want to make your own "Deer" shirt for your parents? (Parents love homemade gifts!) Here are the easy directions:

1. Get a solid color sweatshirt or T-shirt.
2. Slip cardboard inside the shirt so the paint doesn't soak through.

3. Place the shirt on the floor.
4. Pour fabric paint into a paper plate. Take off your socks and shoes. Ask a friend to help paint the bottom of your foot.
5. Carefully press your foot on the middle of the front of the shirt. (You might practice once by stepping on newspaper.) This makes the deer's head.
6. Clean off your foot.
7. Spread paint on the palms of both hands.
8. Place your hands so the heels of your hands touch the toe parts of your foot on the shirt. These form the antlers.
9. Let the paint dry and give the shirt to someone you love.

As you consider being a smile maker, think about other ways to bring smiles to your family. You could

* ☆ Ask to turn off the TV and plan a family game night.
* ☆ Collect all the Beanie Babies and stuffed animals in your house. Take turns hiding and finding your wild animals.
* ☆ Exchange seats at the dinner table and sit in a different spot.
* ☆ Take a coin walk. As a family, go to the end of the driveway. Flip a coin. Heads means you walk left, tails means you head right. Flip the coin at every corner and see where you end up.

✶ Plan a "Little House on the Prairie" night. Read books by candlelight next to the fireplace.

✶ Organize a family talent show. Dress up in costumes and sing and dance for one another.

✶ Play charades.

✶ Ask your mom to have a Jell-O night. Fill a bowl with cold Jell-O and add marbles. Time each other to see who can pick up the most marbles with their toes in the shortest amount of time. Have a contest to see who can slurp the most Jell-O through a straw.

✶ Have a family slumber party in the living room.

✶ Learn some magic tricks.

Step into Action - - - - - - - - - - - - - - →

Here's a great magic trick that will amaze your family and friends.

Put on a short-sleeve shirt. When no one is looking, use clear Chap Stick to print your name on your forearm. Your arm will look completely normal. Gather your family and say in a dramatic voice, "Being the great magician I am, I want to reveal to you the name of the person who is excused from all chores this coming week." Wave your arms, and then sprinkle a small amount of flour over your forearm. Shake off the excess, and your name will appear in white letters on your arm! Of course, you still may have to do chores, but your family will wonder how your name appeared on your arm.

In our house we always try to make the best out of every situation. Sometimes we get very creative being smile makers! My mom is a speaker and sometimes has to be gone for one or two days at a conference. I miss her even though I know she won't be gone long. Sometimes I even cry when she leaves. One time my dad and I had just left the airport to drop off my mom for a short business trip. As we were driving home, my dad decided that when we came to pick up my mom we would dress up as famous characters. Soon the sadness of her leaving faded away. Instead of missing her, I was thinking of all the possible costumes we could wear.

When my mom finally did come home, I was really, really excited about dressing up as Dorothy from the *Wizard of Oz*. My dad and I dug through the costume box and found a blue and white checked dress. We put a stuffed dog in a basket to resemble Toto. I was all decked out, but what would my dad wear? He ended up going as the scarecrow in overalls and a plaid shirt. But what's a scarecrow without straw? We took the straw from our sheep's shed and stuffed it up his sleeves and around his neck. We both looked great when we paraded into the airport lobby. And when my mom got off the airplane, she was certainly surprised—and she certainly had a smile on her face.

My dad and I had so much fun dressing up that we decided to keep trying new costumes whenever we went to the airport to pick up my mom. Once my dad dressed as the Phantom of the Opera. I was Christine, the singer at the theater where the Phantom lived. My dad had a wet paper towel on half his face because he couldn't find a Phantom mask. I was dressed in a fancy opera dress. When my mom got off the airplane, I started singing one of the songs from the musical in a very high voice.

Another time I wanted to dress up as Peter Pan. My dad and I made a costume out of green felt and added green tights and a green hat. Then we went to a thrift store to get my dad a Captain Hook costume. We looked great! This time when my mom got off the plane, we pretended to "battle" each other.

Once we dressed up as bike riders and rode our bikes inside the airport terminal. Another time we went as Tarzan and Jane. We really have fun dressing up in these costumes. When I was younger it helped me get over my mom leaving. Now it's just a fun tradition. Instead of being embarrassed and wondering what people think about our costumes, I think about how much my mom looks forward to seeing us decked out. She left on a trip a few days ago. I wonder what we'll dress up as this time?

Being a Good Friend

We've talked about being a fun person around your family. Now here are some specific ideas for being fun around friends your own age. Whether you have a whole group of friends you hang out with or you have just one or two special friends, friendship is important. Sharing dreams with a close friend is fun. Telling jokes or eating ice cream is more special if you do it with your friends. As with almost everything, friendship takes some effort. You can't just sit around and say, "Okay, friends, make me happy!" The more you are a good friend, the more others want to be your friends too. Here are four ways to be a good friend.

1. *Be interested in your friends.* Let's pretend you see your friend at school wearing a hat. She says, "You'll never believe what happened! I got the worst haircut in the world! I'll never take off this hat!" Think about how your friend is feeling. She needs you to listen to her and be interested in her. So try not to focus on yourself. Do *not* say, "I remember one time I was getting a haircut and the beautician was blowing bubbles with her gum. The bubble popped and got stuck in my hair!"

Good friends show they are interested in others by asking questions about such things as their family or what they did over spring break. Sure, you probably want to tell what you did over vacation, but let others share first. You'll have a chance to share later. Ask your friends for their ideas. If a friend is redecorating her room, ask to see the wallpaper she picked out. Encourage a friend if he or she is running for a school office.

2. *Contribute to the friendship.* Have you ever worked on a school project with five other kids? You're all supposed to put in an equal amount of work, but some kids goof off. You end up doing the majority of work. How does that make you feel? In the same way, friendship involves teamwork. Did your friend decorate your locker for your birthday? Then plan on doing something special on her birthday. Initiate fun things to do together. You don't need to wait until a friend does something for you before you do something. Send a friend a card for no reason. Offer to help if she is having trouble with homework. Be with a friend when she has to baby-sit her younger brother. Buy a "Best Friend"

★Real Life Example from Sondra★

My mom and I decided to have a mother-daughter craft party. We invited ten girls and their mothers to come to our house to make crafts together. It was fun spending time with my friends but also fun being with the other moms. Some of them got very serious about their craft projects, while others just had fun and made crazy things with the supplies. It was work setting up and then cleaning up all the crafts, but we had so much fun it was worth it.

If you'd like to do a craft party, ask an adult to order a catalog from a company like S & S Worldwide (www.ssww.com), either online or by phone: 800-243-9232. They have great craft kits complete with all the materials (paint, fabric, beads, etc.) you'll need. They even have a line of Christian crafts so you can make WWJD jewelry.

bracelet and exchange halves. Invite some friends over for an arts and crafts party. Think of what you can do to make your friends smile.

3. *Be a good listener.* God gave us two ears and one mouth. That must mean we should listen twice as much as we talk! Look at people when they talk to you. Isn't it annoying when you're talking to someone and her eyes are scanning the area

for other friends? It makes you feel unimportant. So set a good example by giving people your full attention. Try not to interrupt your friends. We all want to throw in our witty comments, but sometimes it's good to let your friend finish talking. I saw a T-shirt that said, "Lord, keep your arm around my shoulder and your hand over my mouth." Now that's good advice from a T-shirt!

Step into Action

The next time you are with your friends, try this experiment. See if you can be with them without talking about yourself once. It's hard! If someone says, "I got this great new dress yesterday," you will probably want to say, "I got a cool dress for my birthday." Don't talk about yourself. When the friend mentions her new dress, ask, "Where did you get it?" or say, "It looks really good on you." This may sound easy, but try it. You'll be surprised how hard it is to keep the conversation away from yourself.

4. *Choose friends wisely.* Some people might want to be friends with you, but they make you feel uncomfortable. Perhaps they constantly cut others down, or maybe they call you every fifteen minutes for no reason. They get mad when you need to study for a test instead of going to the movies with them. They might be rude to your parents. These are not the people you want to hang out with.

Real friends are the type of people who are positive, kind, and trustworthy. They think about other people and usually make you smile.

Which of these are characteristics of a good friend?

★ She thinks she is the Queen of Everything.

★ She tries to get good grades in school.

★ She brags about every little accomplishment.

★ She gets mad over little things and holds a grudge.

★ She has a positive attitude.

★ She cheers you up if you're sad.

★ She complains all the time.

★ She helps you study for tests.

★ She tries to get you to skip class.

★ She makes snide comments during the church service.

★ She is trustworthy.

★ She makes others feel bad about themselves.

★ She is involved in extracurricular or volunteer activities.

★ She is a smile maker.

I asked some of my friends about what makes a good friend. Here's the list of characteristics Katy, Alyssa, Alex, Natasha, Anna, Taryn, Mandy, Krista, and Leslie came up with:

funny	caring
sweet	friendly
good listener	thoughtful

59

enjoys the same things as you	always there to help you
respectful	interesting to be with
positive attitude	active
cool	trustworthy
adventurous	honest

More Ways to Be a Smile Maker to Your Friends

Write a cute poem about them.

If you read a book you think they'll like, share it with them.

Plan a trip to a museum or play together.

Do volunteer work together.

Pass a note to them (not too often!) in class.

Being a smile maker isn't hard. Most of the time it simply means thinking about other people and asking, "How can I make them smile?" Instead of having other people try to make you smile, go out of your way to see what you can do to add a smile to their faces.

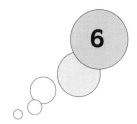

Go the Extra Mile

I saw a poster that said, "There isn't much traffic on the extra mile." I think that means that most people don't give that extra "oomph" to be *extra*ordinary instead of just ordinary. It's easier to do just what is expected, but successful people know they need to go the extra mile to reach their dream.

Describe your favorite meal. How about a pizza dripping with cheese? Add a few pieces of pepperoni and some olives. A cold, refreshing glass of milk washes down the pizza. Include a Caesar salad, and your meal is almost complete.

For dessert add a piece of pie with whipped cream and strawberries. Now that's a meal.

Or would you like a piece of pizza crust and a glass of water?

I know I'd enjoy eating the first meal! A bare-bones meal consists of pizza crust and water. An extra special meal is pizza, salad, and pie.

Why am I talking about food? Because, believe it or not, it relates to being successful. To be successful, you have to do more than just the bare minimum. If your teacher asks for a 100-word report, how about writing 150 words and adding a picture? Sure, it's harder to do more work, but it will get you a higher grade and you'll learn more.

Have you ever used these excuses to procrastinate?

A meteor hit my house and crushed the violin I was going to use for practice.

I had to sharpen one hundred pencils before doing my homework.

I had to file my fingernails and toenails.

I was busy watching the moss grow on the roof.

I decided to read the dictionary from cover to cover.

I folded my socks into perfect triangle shapes.

I had to count all the cracks in my garage ceiling.

My dog ate my homework.

I was forced to watch TV because I couldn't find the remote to turn off the TV.

I wanted to see how many marshmallows I could stuff in my mouth.

Try to get in the habit of doing something "extra." Usually it's just plain laziness that keeps us from giving extra effort. Procrastinating is easier than working to get the job done.

Diamond Excell is an eleven-year-old girl who knows what it is like to try harder than normal. She doesn't have the luxury of procrastinating. Diamond was born without arms and shoulders, which of course makes doing ordinary tasks difficult. How would you tie your shoes if you didn't have hands? How would you hold a pencil? What if you wanted to read a book and turn the pages? Diamond put forth extra effort to live a normal life. She wrote book reports and ate meals using her feet. She even took first place in the handicapped division of the U.S. Open Karate Championships at Disney World.

Diamond's hard work and determination paid off when Ivan Yeager, an inventor, saw her. He used the ideas from his seventh-grade science project to build her bionic arms. They were almost "robot arms," electronically animated down to the fingertips. He spent six months and seventy thousand dollars building the arms. Now Diamond can do things much easier than before. That's a dramatic story of two people giving above-average effort to achieve their goal. Most of us have never had to make the extreme efforts that Diamond did, but when we do make that little extra effort, it helps in the long run.

Think about it: If Diamond didn't put in the extra effort to learn karate, Ivan Yeager never would have met her and never would have made her the bionic arms. Extra effort helped Diamond lead a full life. Now let's see how much it can help you!

Step into Action - - - - - - - - - - - - - - ➤

Do your parents ever tell you how they had to walk twenty-five miles to school in three feet of snow . . . barefoot? Ignore that story, but do ask your grandparents about a time they had to work extra hard to reach a goal. They'll have inspiring stories about ways they overcame problems by giving extra effort to reach a goal.

Sometimes a little extra effort produces dramatic results. Samantha Smith was a ten-year-old American girl who wrote a letter to Yuri Andropov, a former leader of the Soviet Union, when it was called the Soviet Union.

Samantha simply asked if he thought there was going to be a war between the Soviet Union and the United States. He not only wrote back, he invited her family to visit the Soviet Union. She was treated to parades, parties, and dancing in her honor. That simple letter gave Samantha worldwide recognition. Soon she was speaking to children around the world, encouraging them to keep peace in their neighborhoods and in the world.

There are many ways to go the extra mile to achieve success. Have you ever watched Jackie Stiles play basketball on television? While she loved basketball, people told her she'd never play on a major team because she attended a small high school. They felt she wouldn't get "discovered." Jackie went on to become the NCAA all-time leading woman's scorer. She had talent yet also gave extra effort. At five years old, she'd go to the gym and shoot baskets while her dad worked out. As a teenager, she made one thousand shots a day to improve her game. Sometimes she got up at 5:00 A.M.

to lift weights. Who do you think would be a better basketball player? Someone who practices shooting a thousand
baskets and lifts weights or someone who shows up late to
practice and does the bare minimum? Jackie gave extra effort
that paid off.

Begin thinking about ways to give extra effort in what
you do. If your teacher asks you to read five pages in your
history book, you don't have to read fifty-five pages. You
could read the five pages, look at the review questions, and
carefully read the captions under the pictures. That small
amount of extra effort will likely make a difference in class
the next day. It's easy to get lazy and do just what we have
to do. Has your mom asked you to clean your room and
you put just enough things away so she says it's in decent
shape? Why not try giving extra effort by vacuuming your
room or sorting out your books?

Step into Action

This activity might be difficult to do. For one thing,
it will have your parents wondering just what you
are up to! For the next week, give your chores a bit
more effort than you normally do. If you're
supposed to set the table, fold the napkins in a
special way or ask to use candles as a centerpiece.
Are you supposed to feed the dog? Do it before
your mom has to remind you. Wash out your dog's
food and water bowl. Find a plastic mat to put
under your dog's bowl to keep spills off the floor.

Thomas Edison said, "Genius is 10 percent inspiration and
90 percent perspiration." You can be very smart, creative, and

Prudential Spirit of Community Award

Sometimes people ask, "How come you get to do so many exciting things?" My parents have always taught me to take advantage of opportunities. If we hear about a community talent show coming up, I'll go audition. Maybe a group needs people to serve dinner at a homeless center. We'll go help. My agent, Linda Konner, sent me a book called *Catch the Spirit*. It describes kids that won the Prudential Spirit of Community Award. This award is given to adults and youth who do things to improve their community or the world. Many of the people had a dream and worked hard to reach that dream. Each year, around 24,000 students apply.

One girl my age raised money to buy bulletproof vests for police dogs. Another girl collected suitcases so foster kids would have a place to put their things as they moved around. After reading their inspiring stories, I decided to apply. The application had many questions to answer. It took time to get it completed. Then my school principal signed the form and sent it in. I forgot all about it until one morning my dad said, "You might want to read the paper." I glanced down and saw my picture with "Bellingham Girl Shares Top State Volunteer Award." I had won for

(continued on page 67)

Washington State! Each state picks one middle school and one high school winner. We get an all-expense paid, four-day trip to Washington D.C. I also get a medal and $1,000. I'm excited to go on the trip and also excited about the money. I'm going to send part of it to Africa so the kids I met can have a special party.

Have you done something to improve your community? If so, check out www.prudentialspiritofcommunity.org

Take the time to fill out the application and see what happens. You could win a dream come true trip to Washington D.C. and let more people know what great things you are doing with your life.

talented, but unless you give that extra effort, it won't matter. You might think you don't have time to do anything extra. After all, you have homework, youth group, Girl Scouts, basketball, and dance class. Sometimes you need to cut back on doing a lot of activities and concentrate on only a few. Could you be a better basketball player if you had more time to shoot hoops with your dad in the driveway? Consider dropping a few activities. When you don't feel rushed, you can give extra attention to what you *are* doing instead of thinking about what you have to do next.

You have many chances to work a little harder, to give more effort. It is as simple as flossing your teeth after you brush. That's extra effort. Hannah Thomas did more than floss her teeth. She applied for a research scholarship with the Girl Scouts to do research in Antarctica. It meant getting good grades along with filling out lots of paperwork. Hannah felt the skills and the value to always do her best that she learned in Girl Scouts helped her get the scholarship. For ten weeks she visited penguin colonies and lived in a dormitory. Temperatures were far below zero. Hannah said, "Opportunities pop up everywhere—you just have to grab them." Hannah made an extra effort to grab the opportunity to go to Antarctica. Can you make an extra effort to learn a new skill, enter a contest, or improve your grades?

7

When the Going Gets Tough . . .

Have you heard the saying, "When the going gets tough, the tough get going"? You've probably heard, "If at first you don't succeed, try, try again." These two quotes apply to any goal you want to reach. You need to keep trying even if you do run into problems or awkward situations.

Let's say you want to be a professional horseback rider and trainer but your parents don't think a horse would fit in your apartment. Should you just give up and say, "There's no way I can ever reach my goal of training horses"? That's the easy thing to do. Instead, look at other possibilities.

Find a horseback riding stable close to where you live.

Save money to go to a summer riding camp.

Read books about training horses.

Check into leasing a horse from someone who doesn't have time to ride their own horse.

If you know someone with a horse, ask if they'll give you riding lessons in exchange for you cleaning their barn. (Yes, sometimes reaching a goal means shoveling horse poop!)

Often, working toward a goal means you'll run into disappointments. You might not make the team or win the art contest you entered. Maybe your computer will crash when you are doing research for your project. Your little brother might scribble in your poetry journal. Maybe you won't be selected to sing a solo for the church kids' choir. Any of those experiences could upset you and make you want to forget about trying again.

★Real Life Example from Sondra★

A few weeks ago I decided I really wanted a horse. My mom agreed to horseback riding lessons, and my dad agreed to getting me a horse. Well, sort of. My dad went to the garage, got a ladder and some tools, and set to work "making" me a horse in my bedroom. We fastened a board to the wall and attached the other end to the ladder like the back of a horse. It was actually fourteen hands high! I used a pillow for a saddle and could actually sit on my life-size horse in my bedroom. Of course it didn't stop me from still asking for a real horse.

Have you read *Fudge, Sheila the Great,* and *Freckle Juice?* Judy Blume, the author of those books, endured two years of getting her manuscripts rejected before her first book was published. Just think how she felt when she kept getting her stories returned to her with rejection letters. She probably wanted to throw her work away and forget about being a writer. But Judy felt her stories were good, so she kept sending them out. I'm glad she did, because now we get to read all her great books.

Next time you get discouraged, try some of these ideas:

Take a break. Go for a walk or call a friend. Do something to take your mind off the situation. Listen to your favorite music.

Ask God for guidance. Maybe he has some other plans. Have you heard the saying, "When God closes a window he opens a door"?

Ask an adult for suggestions about what to do.

Do something totally unrelated to your goal like cleaning your closet or looking for animal shapes in the clouds.

Keep a positive attitude. Tell yourself, "I have a good idea. I'm working toward my goal. I can come up with creative ideas to reach my goal."

People remember Babe Ruth as a great baseball player. Babe said, "Never let the fear of striking out get in your way." Everyone strikes out at one time or another in reaching his or her goal. Keep trying!

Step into Action

The next time you get discouraged, make a list of all the skills and talents you have. List things like: make friends easily, can spell well, know how to use a computer better than my parents, am a good singer, and so on. Focusing on what you *can* do will help you move forward.

My list of accomplishments:

1.
2.
3.
4.
5.
6.
7.
8.
9.
10.

Many of you have heard about the Chicken Soup books. You might even own a copy of *Chicken Soup for the Pre-Teen Soul.* The authors, Jack Canfield and Mark Victor Hanson, wrote their first book, *Chicken Soup for the Soul,* and sent it to a publisher. It was rejected. They sent it to another publisher. Again, it was rejected. In fact, they sent the manuscript to over one hundred publishers—with no luck. They even printed some copies of the book themselves and passed it out at a book convention. Finally, a small publishing company agreed to publish the book. Well, the Chicken Soup books have sold millions and millions of copies. Among many others they have *Chicken Soup for the Christian Soul*, *Chicken Soup for the Gardener's Soul*, and even *Chicken Soup for the Prisoner's Soul*. If Mr. Canfield and Mr. Hansen had given up after their first rejection, millions of people wouldn't have read all those great stories.

Karen Thorndike was the first American woman to sail around the world through the Great Capes: Cape Horn, Cape of Good Hope, Cape Leeuwin, Southeast Cape, and Southwest Cape. For ten years she planned and dreamed about her thirty-three-thousand-mile sailing trip. Here's what she said about the chance of failure: "The most important thing for me was not whether I accomplished it or how the story ended. Going out there and trying was the most important thing."

When I was nine, I entered a Christian talent show. My act was a humorous monologue. We drove to Tacoma for the first round of competition. As the other contestants began singing and dancing, I felt awkward because of my act. All the singers sang Christian songs like we sing at church. I was doing a monologue about Cinderella's stepsister! My costume was an outlandish dress with huge bows. I had feathers in my hair and polka-dot tights. Everyone else in my age group wore nice "church" clothes. My parents and I hadn't realized that this talent show was geared to display songs or skits you normally hear in church. I love singing in the children's choir at my church, but we thought this talent show was open to all types of talent.

Did I feel like I wanted to leave? Yes! I decided to compete even though I certainly got some strange looks from the other contestants. The funny thing is, I won in my age group! That meant I could compete the following week at the Seattle Center in front of hundreds of people. We had to do our same act, so there I was, a week later, looking like one of Cinderella's ugly stepsisters around everyone dressed in normal clothes.

The Seattle Center was filled with people watching the talent. There were several Christian rock and roll groups. One group of dancers danced to "Amazing Grace." Then I tromped on stage to begin my monologue of complaining about how hard it is to be Cinderella's stepsister. Usually people laughed throughout the whole act, but when I looked at the audience, all I could see were polite smiles. They didn't know what to think of me! As you can guess, I only got fourth place in my division. My first reaction was to say, "I'm never competing again. I'm a failure! I can't act!" (Obviously, I like to be dramatic.)

After getting a large ice cream cone and walking around by the Space Needle, I calmed down. My parents and I talked about how we should have done more research about the talent show. My act was great; this particular talent show was just the wrong place to perform it. My stomach was upset for several hours afterward, but I finally understood. And, yes, I still perform my Ugly Stepsister routine!

Everyone has setbacks when reaching a goal. The main thing is to learn and try again. I learned I needed to get a new monologue that worked for Christian groups! Colossians 3:23 says, "Whatever you do, work at it with all your heart, as working for the Lord, not for men" (NIV). Keep working to reach your goal, because you never know when things will start to "click."

Step into Action - - - - - - - - - - - - - - →

Ask an adult to tell you about Erma Bombeck. (In the rare chance an adult doesn't know, Erma was a very funny writer who wrote newspaper columns and books about her everyday life. Erma published fifteen books and even appeared on the cover of *Time* magazine.) Check out one of her books from the library. An adult will probably tell you how successful Erma was, yet Erma had many problems, including cancer and kidney failure. When Erma failed, she said, "I'm not a failure. I failed at doing something. There's a big difference."

Just because you didn't make first chair in orchestra or score the winning home run doesn't mean you are a failure. Did you learn from the effort? Do you know what to do next time?

The following chart shows positive and negative ways to handle failures.

Negative	Positive
Tell yourself, "I can't do this."	Tell yourself, "I need to keep trying."
Blame your coach, parents, or teacher	Take responsibility for what happened.
Get lazy; don't try.	Keep practicing and working hard.
Quit if accomplishing your goal gets hard.	Keep trying and ask for help.

Last summer I went to a conference in Dallas and heard a speaker by the name of Jamie Clark. No, he's not any relation to me, although my last name is Clark. When Jamie was my age, around twelve, he set a goal of climbing Mount Everest. As an adult, he made his first climb to the top of the mountain—and failed. His team had to turn around about three thousand feet from the summit of Mount Everest.

He tried a second time but failed again.

Jamie tried to figure out why both expeditions had failed even though his team had good equipment and training. Finally, he realized the problem: the team didn't work together; they argued. They even got into arguments about toilet paper. Yes, toilet paper. The team disagreed about how much toilet paper each person could use, and some people even started hiding toilet paper in their pockets so they wouldn't have to share. Because they didn't work together, they couldn't reach their goals.

Jamie's team also fought over food. When people are at extremely high altitudes, their bodies start craving salt. This meant that everyone wanted potato chips. But what happens to bags of potato chips at the bottom of a backpack filled with heavy climbing equipment? (They get crushed.) So then the team fought about who was to blame for all the smushed up potato chips.

On Jamie's third try up Mount Everest, he did bring plenty of potato chips. And this time they didn't get crushed. Can you guess what kind they were? (If you guessed Pringles, you were right.)

Jamie worked hard to get his team working together so they could reach their goal. He had problems, but he kept thinking of new solutions and trying new brands of potato chips!

Another person who kept trying was Anthony Faison. He was convicted of shooting a cab driver and was sentenced to life in prison. The problem was, Anthony was innocent. When he got to prison, he noticed that other prisoners were taking out their frustrations by mistreating and even stabbing other prisoners. Anthony decided to use his frustration in a positive way—he wrote letters asking for help in proving his innocence. Anthony wrote twenty letters a day to anyone he thought could help him. He wrote to the president, to lawyers, and to members of Congress. Over thirteen years Anthony wrote more than sixty-two thousand

Can You Guess Who This Person Is?

He was a partner in two failed businesses.

His fiancée died.

His doctor said he had mental problems.

He liked politics yet lost races to become a state legislator, Congressional representative, U.S. senator, and U.S. vice president.

(And you thought you had problems!)

This person was Abraham Lincoln! He kept trying even when he experienced rejection and failure. So the next time you get upset at not reaching your goal, think about Abraham Lincoln.

letters! He showed great persistence, and it paid off. After thirteen years, a letter he wrote to a detective got results. The detective, Michael Race, read Anthony's letter and then spent two years working on the case. Anthony received a new trial and was proven innocent.

Manners Work Magic

A sk a grandparent or older adult if he or she ever took cotillion classes. *Cotillion?* What's that?

Back in your grandma's day, many kids between the ages of ten and thirteen took cotillion lessons. These were classes designed to turn children into "proper" young ladies and gentlemen.

If you attended a class, you'd learn how to

* ★ slow dance with a boy
* ★ have a polite conversation at dinner (no talking about pimples)
* ★ use a salad fork and soup spoon properly
* ★ wear white gloves and shake hands at formal events

If this sounds interesting to you, many hotels are now offering classes in cotillion subjects. Instead of having to go through the agony of actually slow dancing with a boy, just read this chapter and get "cotillion in a book."

Good manners will go a long way in helping you to be successful. Many businesses now require employees to take classes in manners because so few people know the basics of common courtesy. Let's look at four areas of good manners.

First Impressions

You never get a second chance to make a good first impression. Let's say you were attending a middle school youth group meeting for the first time. As you walked in the door, you saw everyone praying. What type of first impression would you make if you said, "Hey everybody! I'm here! Where's the action? I thought we were here to play games!" Even if you came back the next week and acted appropriately, the other kids would always have that first negative impression in their minds. That's an extreme example, but it does show that people often judge you by the first impression you make.

Here are tips on making a positive impression with adults or kids your own age.

Be Polite

Being polite sounds obvious, doesn't it? Yet kids often forget the basics of politeness. This means saying please and thank you, even to friends. Which would you rather hear? "Katy! Give me that book right now," or "Katy, may I please look at the book when you're done?"

What if your dad made a special trip to the store to get some markers you needed for a school project? Should you say, "Dad, you got the wrong kind. I wanted the scented markers. Now my project is ruined"? Or would this be better: "Dad, thanks for getting me the markers. I'll use them on my project right away"?

Eye Contact

When you meet someone for the first time, look directly at the person. Introduce yourself and smile as the person tells you his or her name. Some people, when meeting someone for the first time, concentrate on the person's eye color. This keeps them looking directly at their new acquaintance.

Think back to the beginning of the last school year. What first impression did your teacher make? Did she walk into the room with a big smile and say something like, "Hi, class. I'm Mrs. Chapman. I hope we'll all work together to make this a fun and productive year together. We'll be learning and laughing together"?

If that's the case, you probably were looking forward to school each day, weren't you?

But if your new teacher strode into the room and glumly said something like, "I hope you all behave this year. Get out a paper and pencil and write a five-hundred-word essay about why school is important. No spelling mistakes allowed," your first impression wouldn't have been so positive.

Just like teachers make a first impression on you, you make a first impression on others too. So the next time you meet someone, give a smile, say hello, and start the relationship on a positive note.

★Real Life Example from Sondra★

If you do have a great teacher, express your appreciation. When I was in fifth grade, I had a wonderful teacher named Mrs. Offutt. When I heard about a contest to find the best teacher, I entered an essay. Here's what I wrote:

Have you ever had a teacher take you to Disneyland for a trip? Have you ever had a teacher give you a new TV if you got 100 on your math test? Have you ever had a teacher who takes your artwork and has it professionally framed? I haven't! I do have a fifth-grade teacher who makes ordinary things seem special. For example,

1. Mrs. Offutt makes art an adventure. Instead of simply giving us leaves for a project, we go on a walk outside to get the leaves.
2. Kids who are disruptive quietly get sent to another room. This gives her more time with kids who are behaving.
3. We have a couch and pillows in our room so we can sit and relax while reading.
4. When we do good work, she puts it on the school web site.
5. Instead of yelling to get our attention, she rings chimes or quietly says, "May I have your attention please?"

(continued on page 83)

> 6. When someone makes her a piece of jewelry, she wears it more than once, even if it is kid's quality!
>
> Mrs. Offutt doesn't take us to Disneyland or give us TVs, but she does give our classroom a want-to-be-there feeling. Wouldn't you like to have a teacher like Mrs. Offutt?

Treat People with Respect

You've probably heard the Golden Rule: "Do unto others as you would have them do unto you." In a nutshell, that means you should treat people like you want to be treated.

Do you like it when people lie to you? Steal from you? Talk behind your back? Cheat when you play a game together? Are jealous if you get a good grade? No, you don't like being treated that way. So you also need to make sure that you treat people with kindness and respect.

As you can tell from the stories in this book, I like to perform in plays and musicals. I started performing monologues for large groups when I was four years old. At five, I was the youngest cast member of *Fiddler on the Roof* for a summer stock production. Since that time I've been Annie in *Annie*, performed in *Joseph and the Amazing Technicolor Dreamcoat*, and even had a special part written for me as the "Yellow Brick" in *The Wizard of Oz*.

My family attends a large church of about three thousand members. Each year our church presents several large-scale children's musicals. A few years ago I prepared to audition for a part in the Christmas musical. Everyone who wanted to try out was to get a script ahead of time and memorize it. On the day of the auditions, the room was packed with kids. We had to act out the script we had memorized and also had to sing a song. Surprisingly, only about half the group had memorized their lines.

I went up to audition for the main role, the part of a clumsy angel named Trip. I purposely stumbled as I came on stage to show I was in character for the part. As I said my memorized lines, I acted like a confused angel.

The next week I found out I got the lead part of Trip! I had to learn a lot of lines and stage directions, but I worked hard and did my best. Performing before a packed church audience was fun.

Several months later I prepared to audition for the spring musical. I followed the same auditioning procedure, once again memorizing my lines and staying in character. I used all my "professional" skills and felt I did a good job.

Soon I got a call from the musical director. She had good news and bad news for me. The good news was that my audition score sheets were the highest, which meant I qualified for the lead part. The bad news was that she wanted me to consider not taking any speaking part at all and let someone else have the chance to perform. She explained that if this were a professional theater production, I obviously would have the part. However, since it was a church production that encouraged a lot of kids to get involved, she was hoping I would understand the importance of giving someone else the opportunity to be a "star." I understood her reasoning but deep down really wanted the part. It's a great feeling to sing and dance before a crowd. It's even more fun to hear the applause at the end.

I knew that declining the part was the right thing to do. I thought about how excited someone else would be to find out she had the lead. Sure, I get to perform before groups all over the country, but it's special to be part of a performance with your friends. As it turned out, I sang in the group choir and got to be in a dance with two of my best friends. I also learned the importance of thinking about other people.

What's a Thank You Note?

Have you ever received a great gift? Suppose you receive a new outfit from your favorite aunt. As you model the outfit, your mother says, "Be sure to write Aunt Betty a thank you note."

You probably dread writing a note, especially an actual handwritten note instead of e-mail. But think about how your aunt will feel when she gets a letter from you telling her you like the outfit. After all, she went to the store, picked out the outfit, paid for it, wrapped it up, and sent it to you. The least you can do is write a note.

Here's the tricky part. What if Aunt Betty sends you a bright pink plastic backpack shaped like a dinosaur? How do you thank her for that gift? You can't lie, but you can thank her for thinking about you. Tell her it was thoughtful of her to send a gift. If you like pink, mention that you like the color.

For the last five years, I've always gone trick or treating at Western Washington University, a college by my house. The students in the dormitories decorate the halls and dress up. My friends and I go inside the dorms and knock on each door to get candy. Because the doors are so close to each other, we get a lot of candy! One dorm has seven floors, and we collect candy from each floor.

One year I decided to write to the president of the college to thank her for encouraging the students to put on this fun event. She wrote me a nice letter in return and told me she'd share my letter with the students on the Halloween planning committee. Knowing the students would get thanked for their work made me feel good.

Receiving a thank you note from my friends if I've given them a book always feels good. In return, I make sure to send a note when they buy me a present. You can also write thank you notes when someone does something nice for you. You can bet I wrote a thank you letter after Chevy gave us a new truck to use for a year!

Here are some other times to send thank you notes:

★Thank the parents of the children you baby-sit for when they give you extra money for doing a good job.

★Send a note to your summer camp counselor telling her you had a good time.

★Thank your teacher in a note if she stays after school to help you catch up on an assignment.

★Write a note to your mom or dad on Mother's or Father's Day to tell them what great parents they are.

★Surprise people who don't expect a card. Send a note to the mail carrier or the newspaper carrier. You do like to read the comics, don't you?

Step into Action

Write a letter to the mayor or governor. You could even write to the president! Tell this person how you feel about a certain issue. Thank them for doing the work they do. Your parents can help you find the address.

★Real Life Example from Sondra★

When George Bush was elected president, I heard him speak about the importance of reading. I sent him a letter and a copy of my book Wearable Art with Sondra. I also told him I love to read. He wrote me a personal letter back to thank me for my book. So if you see President Bush wearing a decorated T-shirt, you'll know where he got the idea!

Table Manners

If you look through your baby pictures, you're sure to find a photo where strained peas or some other baby food is covering your entire face. There's probably one showing you with spaghetti in your hair. (Naturally your mother saves all those pictures.)

Hopefully your table manners have improved. Tipping a bowl of cereal over your head might not be so cute now.

Some Old-Time Manners

In the Middle Ages, people started shaking hands to show they didn't have a sword or dagger in their hand.

The custom of tipping one's hat began when knights used to flip open their visor to see the other person's face.

In the 1500s forks had only two tines. This was good if a person wanted to spear a piece of meat but made it hard to scoop up peas.

The knights of the Crusades had some strict rules about manners at the table. Persons were not to wipe their greasy hands on their coats but on the tablecloth instead. When they finished eating meat off a bone, they tossed it on the floor.

Whether eating pizza with your soccer team or dining at a fancy restaurant for your birthday, table manners are important. Remember the cotillion class? Here are some rules they'd teach you:

* ★ Don't blow on your food if it's too hot. The people sitting next to you don't want soup sprayed on them.
* ★ Ask people to pass the salt or extra food. Reaching across the table usually results in something getting spilled.
* ★ If you take a bite of something that is totally disgusting, try not to gag dramatically, spit it on the table, and gasp, "Ugh! This is gross!" Instead, quietly spit the piece of food into your napkin.
* ★ Speaking of napkins, always keep one on your lap instead of wadded up next to your plate.
* ★ Last but not least, take small bites and chew with your mouth closed. No one likes "chew it and show it."

Manners Wrap-up

You've probably thought, "Oh, these manners tips are so easy." Just because they are easy doesn't mean you should forget to do them. Good manners help you be a successful person. Perhaps you get a job walking your neighbor's dog. If you arrive late to meet your neighbor and don't even comment on how cute her little Pootsie Shmutzie is, you've made a poor first impression.

Maybe you are meeting with a soccer coach to discuss which team you'll be assigned to. If you interrupt him, burp, and cut down the other girls on the team, he'll certainly not be impressed. He's also less likely to listen to your request to change teams.

Most manners are basically common sense. Think about how you can make other people feel comfortable. What can you do to show respect to someone else? How can you thank someone? Treat people as the Golden Rule suggests!

One of the poems in Gelett Burgess's manual called *Manners for Polite Children* gives good advice:

Interruption

Don't interrupt your father when he's telling funny jokes.
Don't interrupt your mother when she's entertaining folks.
Don't interrupt the visitors when they have come to call.
In fact, it's generally wiser not to interrupt at all.

One final warning before we move on to your next step to success: If you do take a cotillion class, it's probably not a good idea to toss your steak bone on the floor!

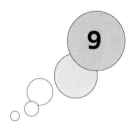

Speaking of Success . . .

When you were a toddler, how did you get a cookie from the cookie jar? Did you scream and wail? Did you sneak over and grab it? Did you say the magic word, "please"? Did you use sign language for "cookie"? Did you smile adoringly at your mother and say, "Cookie"?

As a toddler, you probably communicated in all those ways. Now that you are older, some of those techniques won't work. (However, never underestimate the power of smiling adoringly at your mother!)

One of the best skills you can learn, no matter what you want in life, is how to give a speech before a group of people. Do you get wobbly knees and a yucky feeling in your stomach when you have to give an oral book report in school? All of us are scared to do certain things.

Diana Nyad is an ultra-distance marathon swimmer. She was the first person to swim 102.5 miles from the Bahamas to the shore of the United States. Diana endured twenty-seven hours of hard work, strong ocean currents, and the

There are many ways to communicate. Let's look at a few:

1. Write down your message.
2. Draw a picture.
3. Sing your idea.
4. Show your message with your body.
5. Say what you want.

poisonous sting of jellyfish. She said, "We all have tremendous fear of failure and need to have the courage to try anyway." If Diana can swim nonstop for more than a day, you can give a short speech!

Here are a few tips to help you learn to speak in front of a group with confidence. Who knows? Maybe someday you'll stand in front of a group of businesspeople to ask them for money to help you start your pet-sitting business.

Rule # 1: Prepare—and Prepare Some More!

Can you imagine what it would be like to go in front of your entire school at a talent show to sing a song—without ever practicing? You'd probably open your mouth, see everyone looking at you, and suddenly forget even the first line. Then you'd say those famous last words, "I wish I had prepared!" Sometimes we get the idea we can "fake it," but when giving a speech, it's important to practice ahead of time. Ask your parents to pretend they are the audience. Practice your speech in front of them before you stand in front of your entire class.

Top Ten Scary Things

Can you guess what most grownups are scared of? People's Almanac Presents the Book of Lists shows the top ten fears of adults.

10. dogs
9. tight, closed-up spaces
8. flying in airplanes
7. death
6. sickness
5. deep water
4. money problems
3. spiders
2. heights

And the number one fear is . . .

1. speaking before a group!

Just think—if you get good at public speaking, you have an advantage over most of the adults you know.

Step into Action --------->

Show your friends and family the list of Top Ten Scary Things. Do they agree or disagree with the list? What scares them the most? How do they overcome their fears?

★**Real Life Example from Sondra**★

I was scheduled to give a speech to three thousand people. I practiced in front of my mom and dad, but it didn't seem like a big crowd. I asked the children's church director at my church if I could practice the speech in front of the one hundred kids in my youth group. Practicing in front of a larger "friendly" audience worked great.

Rule #2: Start Out with a Bang

Have you ever been in a boring school assembly where the speaker begins with something like, "Today we're going to talk about the rules for the school jogathon"? Would you want to listen to that for thirty minutes? I don't think so.

But if he started his speech by running back and forth in front of the group and then asked, "How many of you like to run?" he'd have your attention, and you would listen to learn more about his topic.

When you start a speech, be creative. Let's pretend you are standing in front of the class to give a book report. Here are some ways to have an interesting beginning.

★ Ask a startling question: "What would you do if you had to spend the night in a haunted house? [*Pause for dramatic effect.*] That's what happened to the main character in the book I'm going to tell you about." If you want to be really dramatic, you could ask a friend to turn on a tape of spooky music. The public library usually has tapes or CDs of Halloween sound effects.

★ Find an interesting statement that catches the audience's attention. Look under "quotes" on some web sites or find a book listing unusual facts. Let's say you were giving a book report on *The Thank You Book for Kids*, which describes why it is important to have good manners. You might start off your speech with the statement, "In Omaha, Nebraska, if a child burps during a church service, his or her parents may be arrested." That makes people listen!

★ Wear an eye-catching costume or hat. If you're giving a book report on *The Wizard of Oz*, carry a basket with Toto (a stuffed dog) in it. For added effect, put red glitter on a pair of old shoes. (Believe me, teachers love this kind of stuff!) Don't think this is silly. My mother is a professional speaker who has written a book called *Taming the Marketing Jungle*. Guess what she wears when she gives a speech? You're right! A safari outfit with a pith helmet. The audience always loves it.

★ Bring out an unusual prop. If you're doing a report on the book *Cupids Don't Flip Hamburgers*, start the speech by pulling out a cold hamburger from a fast-food bag. In one of my speeches, I show a large pill bottle that contained the malaria pills I had to take before my trip to Africa.

★ During your preparation, write down the main points you want to cover on note cards. This way you can glance down and know what you should say next. Don't worry about memorizing the entire speech. Know it well enough that you can look up at the audience and see their smiling faces.

★ Try to memorize your first four or five sentences so you won't have to look down at your notes. The audience will see your face and feel connected to you.

Think about the ways Jesus spoke to large groups. He always told interesting stories or parables.

Rule #3: Get to Your Main Point

Now that you have everyone's attention, all your preparation will pay off. Are you just giving information? Do you

★**Real Life Example from Sondra**★

I had a class assignment to read a book and do a "creative" book report. That meant I couldn't just write a paper and turn it in. I decided to read Gone with the Wind and write a monologue for Scarlet, the main character. Scarlet was a southern belle, so I made a fancy costume, complete with frilly hat and a ball dress. (I wonder how they ever managed to walk in those huge hoop skirts!) My teacher was impressed by my dressing up as the main character from the book.

want the audience to do something? Pick two or three main points to cover in your speech. If you have eight or nine points, the audience won't be able to keep track of all the information and might get bored. Short and to the point is best. If you're giving a report on *Little Women,* you won't be able to tell about everything that happens to Jo, Meg, Amy,

This would be too much information to include in an oral book review on *Little Women:*

The sisters and their neighbor, Laurie, communicate through a mailbox in their hedge.

Jo burned the back of her dress and had to keep it hidden at the dance.

Jo waited for Aunt March to fall asleep so she could go to the library and read Aunt March's books.

Amy got in trouble at school for trading limes.

Amy fell through the ice and almost drowned.

Jo wrote thrilling stories every night when she was supposed to be sleeping.

and Beth. That's too much information. You could give a short summary of the book and then tell about how the four sisters dress up and participate in their club, The Pickwick Society. The audience will have a better idea about the book from hearing two or three specific situations rather than numerous facts and figures.

Rule #4: The Grand Finale

You might think your speech is over. But wait! There's more! It's time for the curtain call. (Some people call it the end of the speech.) Memorize the last three or four sentences. The ending of a speech is very important because it's the last thing people remember. Be sure to tie in your opening with the ending. Remind the audience about the question or quote you began with. This gives the audience the feeling that you've put time and effort into your presentation.

Finally, get ready to enjoy your standing ovation as the audience yells, "Bravo! Encore! Bravo!"

Being able to speak in front of a group is a skill you'll use all of your life. Because I've done so much speaking and like making crafts, S & S Worldwide asked me to be a spokesperson for their company. They sell arts and crafts kits. Now I'll get to speak to even more people about the fun I have making arts and crafts projects. If you develop your speaking skills, who knows what opportunities will come your way. The sky's the limit!

Step into Action ----------------→

Here's a fun game to play with your family to help all of you improve your public speaking skills. Go through the house and collect five or six really weird items. Do you have a Barbie doll that is missing a head? How about some strange item in a kitchen drawer like a lemon zester? Put all the unique items in a box. One at a time, have a family member reach in the box, select an item, and then try to sell it to the rest of the family. Pretend you are doing an infomercial and say something like this: "Today only, for three easy payments of $23.89, you too can own one of these crushed tissue boxes! Think how lovely your jewelry will look stored in a cardboard box with crumpled sides."

10

Writing Your Way to Success

Remember when you were in kindergarten? You were so proud to print your name! Then you became skilled at writing sentences, and soon you scrawled, "I love Mommy." You were on your way to becoming a writer! Since then, you've probably written many more reports and stories. As you get older, being able to communicate by writing becomes more and more important.

Many people ask me about how I write books. My first two books were on crafts, so I just had to write clear, short sentences on how to do the crafts. With this third book I've had to change the style, because this book uses paragraphs and stories to make a point. Sometimes I dictate things to my mom, who writes them down on paper. Other times my mom will say, "Write a page about a new experience you've had." I write it on notebook paper, and then my mom types it up. I also look up quotes, stories, and facts from other books. I look for books at the library that have interesting information in them. I end up with a notebook full of hand-written pages, magazine articles, and Post-it notes. With hours of organization, all the mess turns into a book!

Whether you write a letter to a pen pal or an article for a magazine, some basic rules of grammar and punctuation apply. The first letter of each heading below forms an acrostic that will help you remember tips to sharpen your writing skills.

Bullet Points Are Great!

I started using bullet points in fourth grade and they always impress my teachers. They are also an easy way to organize your information without writing long paragraphs. Here's a typical paragraph you might write:

My mother has decided that our family needs to eat more healthy foods. She thinks my dad and I eat too many chips and candy bars. In her opinion, for breakfast we should eat grapefruit, wheat toast, and soy milk. Then at lunch our meal should consist of broccoli and lentil soup. Let's not forget the carrots for dessert! Dinner is a wonderful vegetarian pizza . . . with carrot sticks for dessert of course.

Sometimes bullet points convey the message just as well. You could write

My mother has decided that our family needs to eat more healthy foods. She thinks my dad and I eat too many chips and candy bars. In her opinion, we should eat foods like

- grapefruit
- wheat toast

- soy milk
- broccoli
- lentil soup
- carrot sticks

The next time you are writing a list of related items, try putting them in bullet-point format.

Edit Your Work

Sometimes we just want to finish writing and be done with a report or story. We write the last sentence and say, "I'm done!" You'll probably get a better grade if you take some time to edit your work. Look for obvious mistakes. You should check for

- grammatical errors
- punctuation errors
- run-on sentences
- overused words
- neatness
- spelling mistakes

Here's a list of commonly misspelled words. (I've misspelled them all!) I keep this list handy to help me when I write.

believe   necessary
foreign   physical
knowledge   privilege

receive   science
recommend   separate
rhyme

Astound Your Reader

Would you want to read a paragraph like the following?

I went to bed. I had a scary dream. A scary monster scared me. I woke up and was still scared. The End

Think of ways to make your writing interesting. Use descriptive words and add details. Is this easier to read?

After watching a horror movie on TV, I raced up the stairs to the safety of my bed. I hoped for a good night's sleep, but oh, was I in for a surprise! After falling asleep, all of a sudden a humungous four-eyed monster jumped in front of me. He had bad breath and mucus dripping from all four eyes. I was so scared I started throwing my Beanie Babies at him. With a start, I woke up and realized I was throwing Beanie Babies at my dad, who had come in to say goodnight.

Here are other ways to make your writing interesting:

- Use a thesaurus to find better word choices.
- Write picture stories instead of a plain statement. Instead of writing, "I was cold," you could write, "The wind whipped at my nose and frosted my glasses so I couldn't see."
- Have an interesting opening. People don't get too excited about reading a report that starts with "The

104

★Real Life Example from Sondra★

I am a terbul spelr! Have you ever been in a spelling bee? Did you win? If I ever entered a spelling bee, I'd probably lose on the word dog. I can't spell! I use the spell checker when doing work on the computer, but when writing on paper, I really have trouble. Because of my lack of spelling ability, I have to practice and put extra effort into figuring out how words should be spelled.

War of 1812 took place in 1812." Come up with a fascinating statistic or a quote that will make people want to keep on reading.

Work at Your Writing

I saw a program on TV showing a young girl training for a national rhythmic gymnastic competition. She practiced five hours a day! You don't need to write five hours a day, but you should practice. You could keep a journal, write extra-credit reports for school, or even enter writing contests. Many web sites offer opportunities for kids to get stories or articles published. The more you write, the better you'll become.

Remember Basic Writing Skills

You probably learned the basics of writing in elementary school. Those important points will carry you through until college and be useful even when you are a grownup!

I'll use bullet points to remind you of some ways you can easily improve your writing skills.

- Do you capitalize the first letter of every sentence? Don't forget that names of people and places need to be capitalized also.
- Put a period at the end of every sentence. Sure, you'll occasionally add a question mark or an explanation point, but most of the time just end with a period. Period!
- Brainstorm ideas. If you are writing about your summer vacation, first make a list of all the things you did. Once you think of a few activities, others will come to mind.
- Organize your thoughts and ideas. Try to develop a beginning, middle, and end. Reading a report that jumps around from one point to another and back again is difficult.

Interesting Sentence Lengths

Reading sentences that are all the same length is like reading a list—boring. For example, "I have a golden retriever. He likes to fetch his ball. He enjoys playing with me. His name is Fred."

Concentrate on writing sentences of different lengths. You could write, "My horse was running so fast down the trail that I had trouble holding on to the saddle. Then he stopped suddenly." The short sentence provides a contrast and adds more interest to your story.

Has your teacher told you to avoid run-on sentences? Those are sentences run together without proper punctuation. They have so many details they are hard to follow. They look like this: "One day I went to the store but I couldn't find the milk so I got powdered milk instead, even though it was more expensive and I didn't have the extra money so I had to ask my friend Georgia to buy the milk."

Short, to-the-point sentences are easier to understand. Look at your long sentences to see if they can be made into shorter ones.

Step into Action - - - - - - - - - - - - - - →

Here's something you may not have done in a long time. Write a letter! Your grandma or grandpa probably would be thrilled to get a real letter in the mail. Brainstorm about some things you could write about. (Grandparents are easy. They love hearing if you've brushed your teeth.) Make sure you capitalize properly and organize your thoughts. Writing a letter is good writing practice plus it makes your grandparents *very* happy.

Try Different Writing Techniques

As you write letters, stories, or even books, feel free to try different techniques. If you've never written a poem before,

107

why not try one? Usually you think poems need to rhyme, such as that famous Valentine poem:

Roses are red,
violets are blue,
sugar is sweet,
and so are you!

I wrote a rhyming poem that went like this:

Fall
Watch the falling leaves,
Breathe the fresh air.
Think of all that nature holds,
Experience it there.

Many poems are free form, which means they don't have to rhyme. Pick a subject and let your mind flow in short sentences. Here's another example I wrote:

Waterfalls stream down,
Cascading onto the rocks,
And glimmer in the sun.

Keep trying different writing styles. Is your writing style basic and factual? Maybe you write sentences like this: "Katie ran as fast as she could to get home. She didn't want to be late." Try adding some drama to your writing by adding descriptive words. You could change those sentences to: "Katie's braids sailed in the air as her legs propelled her home. Everything hinged on racing the clock so she wouldn't miss her deadline." See how that is more interesting? Certain styles of writing will seem more comfortable to you, but every once in a while, just as a writing exercise, try something different. If you write with a flourish, try sticking to facts. If you like long sentences, see what happens if you write with shorter sentences. Keep writing and keep trying!

End with Interest

As with a speech, people remember the end of your report or story. The ending needs to sum up what you've written. Include a point from your opening paragraph in your closing. This gives the reader a feeling of "coming around the circle." (Some people always read the last page of a book first, so you had better make it interesting.) You

★**Real Life Example from Sondra**★

Our class had an assignment to write a poem using our vocabulary words. Here's the poem I wrote. It has a surprise ending.

He cheeped a pleasant melody
Singing directly to me,
His feathers shone in the sun.
The rhythm of his melody was oh such fun.
One day little Tweety looked in despair.
Could it be something in the air?
He didn't sing from his wooden perch
But instead, fell to the ground with a lurch!

have probably read some of Shel Silverstein's poems. He often has surprise endings.

Read Many Books

Reading a variety of books will help you see how different people write. Fiction is different than reading a book on raising hamsters. Poetry is different than a mystery. The more you read, the better you'll be able to say, "I like that style" or "That book was boring." You don't want to copy other authors, but you do want to know about different writing styles.

★**Real Life Example from Sondra**★

Here's a very short poem I wrote about reading:

Books

Mystery, biography, fantasy, and fiction,
These are a few of my book addictions.

Think about your favorite book. Why do you like it? Does the author use descriptive words? Does he or she keep you guessing about what happens next? Try to add a few new ideas to your own writing. Use a thesaurus to embellish your writing. Look at books you have and read their opening sentences. Then figure out how you can use ideas from other authors to improve your own writing.

One of the best ways to get practice writing is to keep a journal. Try to write in it several times a week. (I always start out thinking I'll write daily, but it never seems to work that way.) Journals are places for you to write about your dreams, problems, and thoughts. And they are a good place to record your goals, because you can always go back and see what you wrote down several weeks ago.

There you have it. BE A WRITER!

Taming the Butterflies

Guess what!" I yelled to my counselor. "I'm going to Africa!"

There I was at Bible camp, getting ready to go water skiing, when a letter arrived from my mom telling me we were going to Africa in December. I thought, *She must be kidding. Isn't Africa where headhunters and cannibals attack eleven-year-old girls? What would I do there?*

As it turned out, Childcare International wanted me to go to Africa to meet the AIDS orphans living in their children's homes. That way, when I gave speeches to churches, I could tell them about my experiences.

On my first day in Africa, I found myself standing up in the back of a pickup truck, holding on as tight as I could, while it raced down an airport runway. This wasn't the type of airport found in the United States. The runway was a grassy field with packed dirt for a landing strip. My hair streamed behind me as the driver put the pedal to the metal on the rough runway. Instead of a seat belt for protection, I had guards with guns standing on both sides of me. I didn't know if they were protecting me from Africa or protecting Africa from me! It felt exhilarating to be bouncing along in the back of a pickup but also scary. Even though my parents were with me, I still felt nervous. A line in *Fiddler on the Roof* says, "I'm a stranger in a strange new place." That described me. Everything was new. People spoke Swahili, while I spoke English. Streets were littered with garbage, and people lived in cow-dung huts. Normally, when I travel in the United States, things are basically the same wherever I go. Even as I visit different churches, I can count on people praying and singing and a pastor preaching. I've gone to McDonald's in the United States, Canada, and Europe. The food tastes the same in all those places!

In Africa everything looked and smelled different. I told myself that the different customs were simply different, not right or wrong. Throughout the entire trip I tried to be positive and to learn from what I was experiencing. I remembered reading about a girl who spent a year traveling around the world with her parents. She kept complaining because every place was not like America. She wanted ice in her drink, and she wanted to hear American songs on the radio. I decided to view my Africa trip as a chance to learn about other people, even if it made me nervous. The more I found out about Africa, the better I could explain the situation to people in the United States. I might be uncomfortable for a few days, but kids in Africa live their whole lives in uncomfortable situations with little food or shelter.

In working toward achieving your dream, you'll find yourself in new situations. It's easy to get scared and give up trying to reach your goal because you are out of your comfort

★Real Life Example from Sondra★

My friend Georgia wrote this example of a time she was scared but decided to take a risk.

When I was about nine or ten, I thought I was a really good swimmer. Sondra decided to teach me how to do a back dive. On my first try I was so scared! I thought I was going to hit the wall when I dove backwards. I finally shook off my fear and tried my first back dive. I dove backwards but didn't actually do a back dive. I kept trying though. Afterwards I did it and didn't feel scared anymore. So if you think something is scary, try to overcome it.

zone. Maybe you decide to improve your soccer skills by going to a residential soccer camp for two weeks. After you sign up, you find out none of your friends are going. Do you back out? It's tempting, but make the effort to go through with your plans. Introduce yourself to other soccer players, ask questions, and get to know the coach.

When I saw the armed guards on the truck in Africa, I wanted to fly straight home. But I smiled and realized they were there for my protection.

Let's imagine you decide to audition for your first community theater production. You'll have butterflies in your stomach. Remember the famous saying, "If you have butterflies in

115

● ● ● ● ● ● ● ● ● ● ● ● ● ● ● ● ● ● ● ●

Melissa Buhl is a champion BMX and mountain bike racer. She performs jumps and maneuvers in bicycle motocross races. She races boys and other girls and has to watch that they don't try to push her off the track. It's a rough sport with lots of speed and action. Sometimes she gets nervous before a race, but she says, "Being confident and aware of your abilities calms you down. It's the first step toward winning." Sometimes it helps to know that other people are nervous too. Think about all your skills and start taking small steps forward.

● ● ● ● ● ● ● ● ● ● ● ● ● ● ● ● ● ● ● ●

your stomach, train them to fly in formation." That means take control and conquer your fear. Say a short prayer asking God for help. Walk into the theater with confidence. Find out where to sign in. Get a script and do your best. Even if you don't get a part, you now know the steps to auditioning for a play.

Part of any new experience is overcoming your fear. It's easy to walk away and go home, but look at what you might miss. You could audition and end up getting the part of Annie!

A Chinese saying goes, "The longest journey starts with a single step." Even if you are nervous about doing something new, try taking a single step. Ask yourself, "What can I do to

Appropriate and Inappropriate Risks

When thinking about taking risks, remember that there are appropriate risks and inappropriate risks.

Appropriate Risks

Run for class president.
Try out for a program such as Math Olympiad.
Write a letter to a celebrity asking for an
        autograph.
Give your testimony at your church.
Start a Bible study at your school.
Enter a contest.
Learn a new hobby.
Sit with someone who is alone at lunch.
Join a new club at school.

Inappropriate Risks

Change your hair color with enamel spray paint.
Let a friend pierce your ears.
Use a hairdryer in the shower.
Jump off a roof when a friend challenges you.
Ride your bike without a helmet.
Unhook your seat belt when riding on the freeway.
Stick your hand in the shark tank at the zoo.
Make a prank phone call.
Try to download a virus onto your computer.
Go skydiving without a parachute.
Try smoking a cigarette.

get over my fear?" Are you scared to start a new school? Could you read a book about someone who went to a new school and made friends?

Step into Action - - - - - - - - - - - - - - - →

Bring out all the family photo albums. Look at your baby pictures. Notice how many things you couldn't do as a baby that you can do now. The pictures probably show you trying to walk or wobbling on your first two-wheel bike. See! You took risks and tried things when you were younger. Now keep on trying, because you can do it!

Recently I participated in a speech contest at the youth program for the National Speakers Association. All 150 kids who were there had parents who were professional speakers like my mom. This meant they knew how to have an effective opening, how to get the audience involved, and how to have an impressive conclusion. Bravely, I entered and won the first elimination. The next day fifteen of us competed again, and I made it to the final round. Then I panicked! I would be competing against eighteen-year-olds! My first thought was to go home. We actually were scheduled to leave that morning, but my mom changed our flight when she knew I was in the final event. My stomach hurt, and I kept telling my mom I couldn't go through with it. We prayed about the situation, but I was still scared.

Everything inside of me said I'd fail miserably at the speech contest. What if I came in last? What if I froze up? I called my dad back home and told him I didn't want to do it. He encouraged me and reminded me of all the speeches I'd given before.

He told me to remember how audiences clapped and smiled for me.

I tried one last time to convince my mom I was too sick to compete. She knew it was a bad case of nervousness. I told her, "The contest is not a big deal. Let's catch our original flight home." Instead, we spent some time going over what would happen. Each contestant would reach into a hat and pull out a made-up word like "groopingplatus." Then he or she would have thirty seconds to mentally prepare a speech before stepping forward and speaking. My mom told me to figure out a way to get the audience involved in my speech. Instead of talking *at* them, I should make them feel like a part of my presentation.

Deciding to simply try and do my best, I went to the contest area but told my mom not to come in. I also thought about Philippians 4:13, "I can do everything God asks me to with the help of Christ who gives me the strength and power" (TLB).

The room was packed with kids from the conference. Six judges were in the audience. Several kids competed ahead of me, and I watched to see how their speeches turned out. I also got some ideas about how to involve the audience.

Suddenly it was my turn. I reached in the hat and got the word *sniffaslime. Sniffaslime?* What was that? I decided to do something completely different from the other contestants. Standing in front of the group, I asked, "How many of you have cats for pets?" Many raised their hands. Then I explained that America was facing a problem: "There are too many fat cats around! But don't worry," I said. "You can help your cat lose weight with this great cat exerciser called the Sniffaslime!" I quickly took off my belt to use as a Sniffaslime.

119

"Let me show you how this works. I'll need a volunteer from the audience to be my cat." I brought up a counselor and had him get on his hands and knees. The audience loved it. I made my "cat" meow, and the audience really laughed. The rest of my speech had the cat jumping over the Sniffaslime, jumping up for it, and doing other silly things. I ended the speech by pointing to the counselor and saying, "See, the Sniffaslime works. Doesn't this cat look thinner than when I started?" People clapped and cheered. I felt great to have done my best. Of course it felt even better when I heard I had won first place!

I never would have had that wonderful feeling of accomplishment if I had given in to my fear. I had asked adults for help and then prepared as much as possible—and it worked!

Think back to the last few years of your life. You've already had many new experiences. Have you ever ridden a horse? Learned to swim? Gone down a steep waterslide? Learned to play an instrument? Sung a solo in a talent show? Participated in a spelling bee? Learned to inline skate? Eaten sushi? See, you've survived all those once scary experiences that seem easy to you now. The point is, new experiences make us nervous.

Here are some ways to overcome your uneasiness in trying new experiences:

Ask an adult for help.

Take a deep breath or do ten jumping jacks.

Have a positive attitude.

Find out as much information as you can about the situation.

Ask a friend for moral support.

Step into Action - - - - - - - - - - - - - - - →

This week try something new. Maybe you could make dinner for your family. Talk to a different group of kids at school. Ask your grandmother to teach you how to knit! By making a conscious effort to try something new, you'll learn to overcome those butterflies that pop up when you are out of your comfort zone. Send me a picture of the great ski sweater you learned to knit!

The next time you are faced with a new situation, just remember me doing the speech about Sniffaslime. If I can figure out what a Sniffaslime is, you can certainly overcome your fear of a new situation!

As you read the ideas and tips in this book, hopefully you'll develop your own formula for reaching your dreams. Just remember, God made you a unique person with your own special style. Now go after your dreams in your own special way!

Twelve-year-old Sondra Clark is the author of *Craft Fun with Sondra* and *Wearable Art with Sondra,* recipient of the national Fox TV Kids Hero Award and the Prudential Spirit of Community Award, speaker for churches and conference groups, and the spokeschild for Childcare International. Sondra's mom, Silvana Clark, is also a published author and frequent conference speaker.

Sondra gives a portion of the proceeds from this book to Childcare International, www.childcare-intl.org

Check out Sondra's web site at www.sondrascrafts.com—you can e-mail her through that site.